Treasure hunters hope to find gold and silver, but archaeologists want to make a map of the site, excavate, find objects which can be **conserved** and make a record of what's there.

Underwater equipment

Underwater **archaeology** is more difficult and expensive than working on dry land. A boat is needed to get to a wreck at sea, and divers to investigate the site. If it's difficult to see underwater, divers have powerful torches to light the way. They use waterproof pens, measuring tapes and cameras to record what they find, and excavate by hand or use a machine called an air lift, which sucks the sand up like a vacuum cleaner. Objects can be lifted to the surface in baskets, or pulled up by cranes if they're really heavy.

a diver using an air lift

Special cranes are used to lift large objects out of the water.

Mini submarines and robots are sometimes used to explore under the water when a wreck is too dangerous for divers. Special cameras and computers record what they find. This robot moves in the same way as a turtle swimming. Its flippers don't disturb the water, so it's easy to get a good look at the objects.

scientists testing the turtle robot

What happens in the water?

Water can damage objects, but it can also **preserve** them. Some materials last longer in water than if they were buried in soil.

Pure gold survives well and still looks shiny, but silver can be damaged.

Glass can be marked.

Wood may look better than it really is. Shipworms (like woodworms) may have eaten some of it before the boat was wrecked! The wood needs to be slowly and carefully dried out and then sprayed with chemicals to make it stronger.

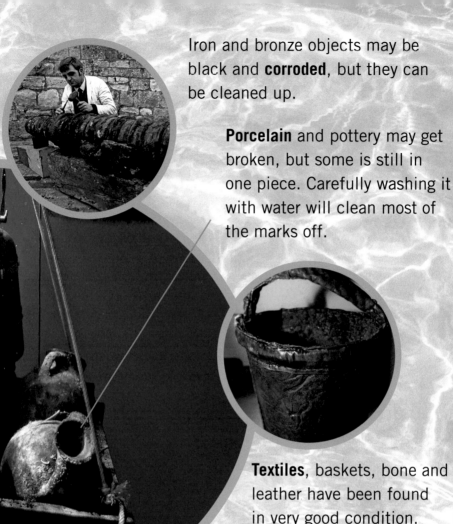

Iron and bronze objects may be black and **corroded**, but they can be cleaned up.

Porcelain and pottery may get broken, but some is still in one piece. Carefully washing it with water will clean most of the marks off.

Textiles, baskets, bone and leather have been found in very good condition. Leather has to be washed several times with very pure water and then **freeze-dried**.

Stone may be worn away by the water, or covered in seaweed and **molluscs**.

Ancient cargo

Ship's log

Location: Turkey
Date: about 1305 BCE
Known as: Uluburun shipwreck

No one knows where this 15-metre-long Bronze Age trading ship was heading, over 3,000 years ago. It's one of the oldest boats ever found and its precious **cargo** was clearly for someone rich and powerful.

This is what experts think the inside of the ship may have looked like.

This is what's left of the boat.

On board, divers found ten tonnes of copper and a tonne of tin, which can be melted together to make bronze. There were 130 clay vases, called "amphora", one packed with beads, and one with olives, 150 bars of coloured glass, 23 stone anchors, weapons, a solid gold **scarab** and seven hippopotamus teeth! The boat never made it to shore, but we now know what kind of luxury goods were being traded at the time.

This solid gold cup was also found in the wreckage.

Tudor treasure

In 1545, one of the most important warships in King Henry VIII's navy sank during a sea battle against the French. Only about 25 of the 400 men on board survived, and attempts at the time to **salvage** the ship failed.

Today, hundreds of objects have been recovered from the *Mary Rose*. Some of them are rare finds, like the 137 bows, but others are everyday objects – such as 85 combs used to get nits out of hair! These tell us all about life in Tudor times, especially on board a ship.

Items found in the wreck were put into special sealed containers and brought to the surface.

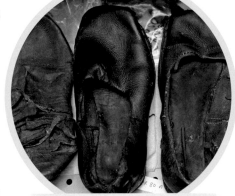

Over 400 shoes and boots were found on the ship.

games board

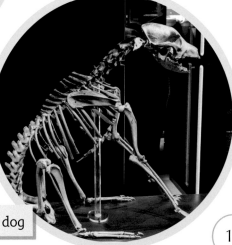

skeleton of the ship's dog

White gold

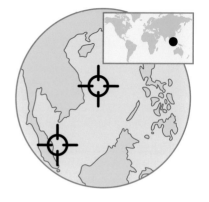

Ship's log

Location: Malaysia (Java Sea)
Date: 1625
Known as: Wanli shipwreck

When Europeans first saw Chinese porcelain they called it white gold. No one in Europe knew how to make it because the recipe was a secret. The porcelain was so beautiful it became a new kind of treasure.

When modern-day fishermen caught the blue and white china in their nets, this led to the discovery of several wrecks filled with white gold. Over 400 years ago, the Wanli ship sank with a cargo of about 700,000 pieces to be sold to rich people in Europe. Over 300 years later, white gold is still worth a lot of money.

Tek Sing was wrecked on a **reef**, leaving 350,000 pieces of white gold on the sea bed.

Ship's log

Location: South China Sea
Date: 1822
Name: *Tek Sing*

Divers had to battle underwater currents, murky water and tropical storms to bring the cargo to the surface.

This is what it looks like after it's been cleaned.

This is what the white gold looked like on the sea bed.

Doggerland

It's not only ships that are found underwater.
Sometimes huge areas of land disappear, like Doggerland.

Britain was once joined to the rest of Europe,
but when the ice sheet melted over 10,000 years ago,
sea levels rose. Land with forests and hills, where thousands
of people had lived and hunted, disappeared under
the waves. Sometimes fishermen nowadays catch
ancient weapons and tools in their nets,
which have floated up from
the drowned land below.

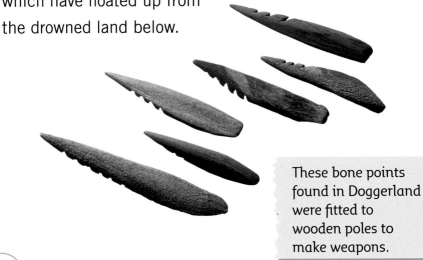

These bone points
found in Doggerland
were fitted to
wooden poles to
make weapons.

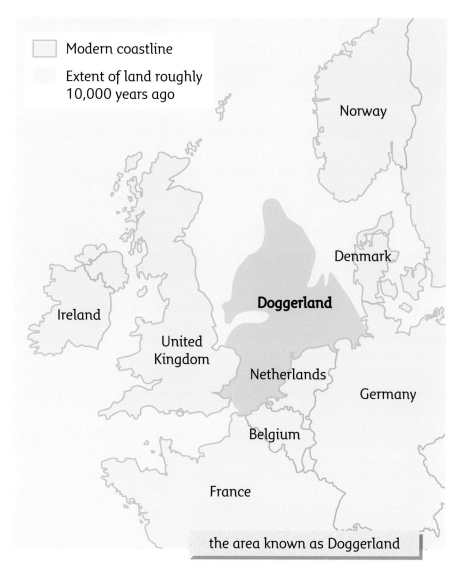

Norway

Denmark

Doggerland

Ireland

United
Kingdom

Netherlands

Germany

Belgium

France

the area known as Doggerland

Experts are now making a map of the sea bed. They're also checking bones and plants recovered there, so we can find out more about the people who lived and died at that time.

Seahenge

Log

Location: Holme beach,
    Norfolk, UK
Date: 2049 BCE

Nearly 4,000 years ago, in the summer of 2049 BCE, a group of people using bronze tools pulled an enormous oak tree into a marshy area, overlooking the North Sea. They buried the tree trunk upside down, so its roots pointed towards the sky. Around the upside-down tree, they placed 55 more oak trees in a circle.

Over time, first sand and then the sea covered the tree trunks. 4,000 years later, as the tide went out, the circle of tree trunks was uncovered. No one knows why it was made or what it was used for, but it may have been a special place for people to meet or make offerings to the gods.

The oak trunks were carefully removed from the sea, and have been preserved.

A lost city

Log

Location: Egypt –
    Mediterranean coast
Date: about 700 BCE
Name: Heracleion

The rich city of Heracleion was destroyed nearly
1,200 years ago, when an earthquake caused it to sink
into the sea. It was a busy port, and trading ships from
all over the Mediterranean unloaded their cargoes in
the harbour. People at the time had written about the city,
but no one knew where it was until divers found it off
the Egyptian coast.

This is what experts
believe the city of
Heracleion looked like.

Under the water were gigantic statues and whole temples, 700 anchors and over 60 shipwrecks. A huge **granite** slab was covered in **hieroglyphs** which spell out the name of the city and information about paying **taxes**.

A strong crane was needed to lift this statue out of the water.

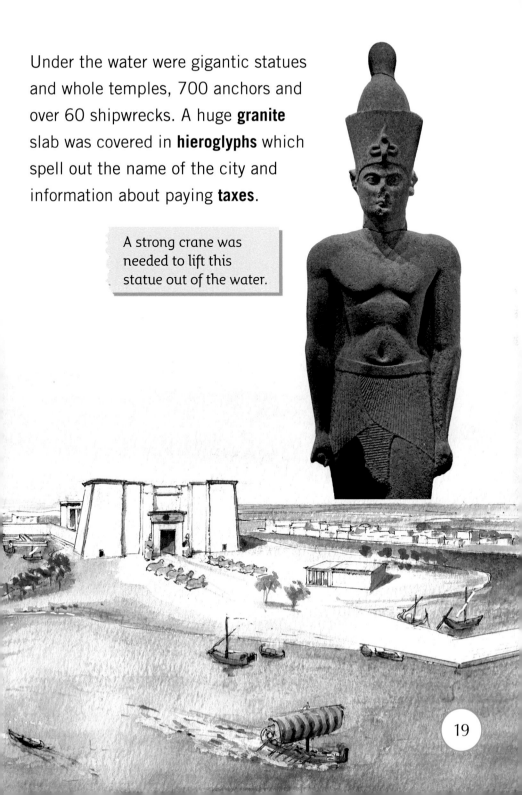

Sword puzzle

Log

Location: River Witham,
   Lincolnshire, UK
Date: about 1250
Name: the Witham Sword

Some underwater finds are a puzzle. Experts have
been trying for 100 years to work out the meaning of
letters on a double-edged steel sword **inlaid** with gold
wire found in the River Witham. The 18 letters are:
NDXOXCHWDRGHDXORVI and if they can be **deciphered**,
they might tell us something about the sword, who owned
it and why it ended up in a river.

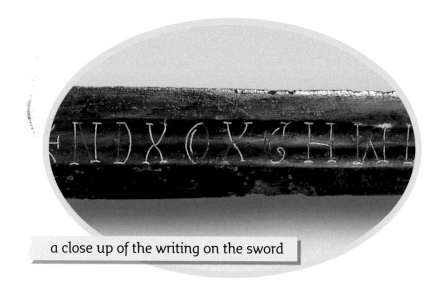

a close up of the writing on the sword

Dozens of swords with writing on them have also been found in Europe. The blades were usually made in Germany. Some of the writing seems to be in a shortened form of **Latin**. Thousands of years ago, weapons like these were thrown into rivers, maybe as an offering to the gods.

the Witham sword

Giants from the sea

Log

Location: Mediterranean, near
    Riace, Calabria, Italy
Date: about 460 BCE
Name: Riace bronzes

There aren't many ancient statues
made of metal that have survived.
In the past, people used to melt
them down and make them
into something else.
But on the sea bed in
the Mediterranean Sea,
two enormous bronze
statues *had* survived.
The statues are over
2,500 years old and
over two metres tall.
Each weighs nearly
a tonne, so lifting them
out of the water by
crane was difficult.

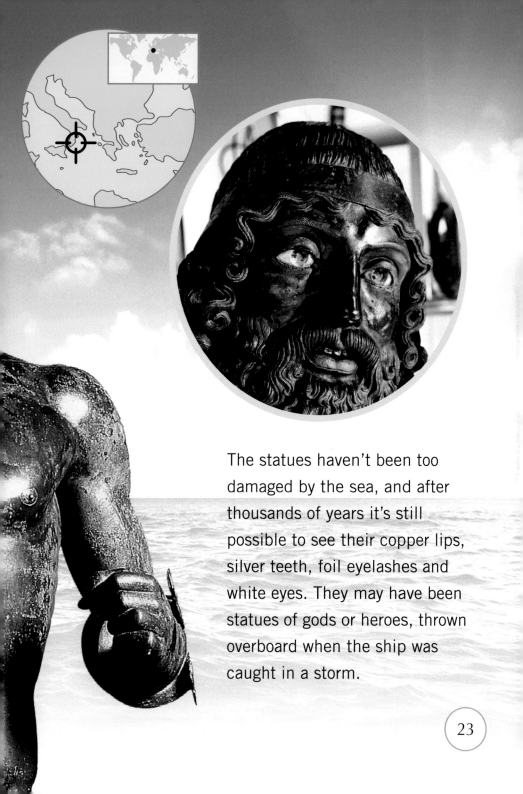

The statues haven't been too damaged by the sea, and after thousands of years it's still possible to see their copper lips, silver teeth, foil eyelashes and white eyes. They may have been statues of gods or heroes, thrown overboard when the ship was caught in a storm.

Foreign gold

Ship's log

Location: Jupiter inlet, Florida
coast, USA
Date: 1659
Name: *San Miguel de Arcangel*

Sometimes treasure is found a long way from where it was first made. Divers excavating the *San Miguel de Arcangel,* which was wrecked off the coast of Florida, USA, found 12,000 silver and gold coins. The coins were on their way from Cuba to the King of Spain.

Since then, divers have been finding lost treasure from other Spanish ships, including gold coins worth millions of pounds. The gold in these ships came from mines in South America.

Spanish gold coins found near Florida.

Location: Salcombe, Devon, UK
Date: about 1650
Known as: Salcombe Treasure

On the other side of the Atlantic
Ocean, ships have been wrecked
off the coast of Devon, in the UK, for thousands of years.
Divers brought up over 400 Moroccan gold coins and
gold jewellery. It may have been an English ship trading
with North Africa or a pirate ship carrying stolen treasure.

finds from the Salcombe wreck

25

Old and new

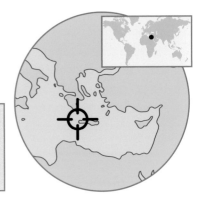

Over 100 years ago, a machine was found under the sea. It had been lying there for about 2,000 years and experts believe it's one of the earliest computers ever made. It could have been used to do sums and possibly **foretell** the movements of the sun, moon and planets. It's still being studied today to find out how the 30 hand-cut bronze **gears** worked. Divers are continuing to explore the sea bed where it was found, hoping to find more parts of the device.

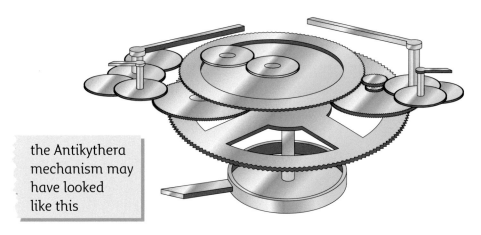

the Antikythera mechanism may have looked like this

Today, it's modern computers and robots that will map and photograph underwater, locating lost treasure. The torpedo robot can dive down to 6,000 metres so, in the future, we'll know as much about what's under the water as we do on land.

the torpedo robot – the future of underwater archaeology

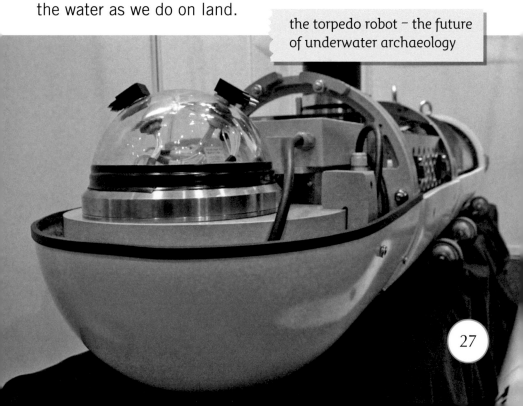

Glossary

archaeologists people who study the past using objects that have been dug up on land or in water

archaeology the study of the past using objects that have been excavated from land and water

BCE before the common era, the same as BC

cargo goods carried on a ship

conserved kept from more damage

corroded worn away, especially metal

deciphered found out the meaning

excavated dug up with care

foretell tell of an event before it happens

freeze-dried make an object very cold, then remove the ice

gears small wheels with teeth

granite very hard rock

hieroglyphs ancient Egyptian writing

inlaid set in to

Latin language spoken and written by ancient Romans

molluscs sea creatures with a shell

preserve keep free from decay

porcelain fine, very hard, almost see-through china

reef rocks near the sea surface

salvage rescue a ship and its contents from the water

scarab ancient Egyptian gem in the shape of a beetle

taxes money paid to the ruler of a town or city

textiles cloth made by knitting or weaving

Index

Lost and found

investigating underwater

shipwrecks

white gold

30

lost worlds

gold

weapons

Ideas for reading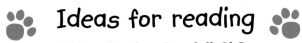

Written by Clare Dowdall, PhD
Lecturer and Primary Literacy Consultant

Reading objectives:
- retrieve and record information from non-fiction
- read books that are structured in different ways
- make predictions from details stated and applied

Spoken language objectives:
- participate in discussions, presentations, performances, role play, improvisations and debates

Curriculum links: History –historical enquiry; Geography – geographical skills; Art – creativity

Resources: collage materials; atlas, globe or ICT, paper and pens.

Build a context for reading

- Tell children the title of the book and ask them to suggest what sort of "treasure" might be found under water.
- Hand out the books and read the title and blurb. Ask children to discuss what they can see in the image, and describe any underwater treasures that they have found.
- Turn to the contents. Read through and ask children to predict what each heading might be about, as preparation for reading, e.g. what does the name "Seahenge" remind them of?

Understand and apply reading strategies

- Turn to pp2–7. Read the text together and discuss the meaning of unfamiliar vocabulary. Model how to use the glossary to seek a precise definition.
- Discuss what is happening in the image on pp2–3. Develop children's vocabulary by using introducing technical language as they discuss their ideas, e.g. SCUBA equipment, breathing apparatus, terracotta pot, treasure.